QUICK STICK HARRY and THE BALL HOG

A Quick Stick Harry Series

JOHN R SARDELLA

Tellwell Talent
www.tellwell.ca

ISBN
978-0-2288-4495-2 (Hardcover)
978-0-2288-4494-5 (Paperback)

This book is dedicated to those
who love this great game.

Quick Stick Harry jumped out of bed. Today was the big game! It was the lacrosse championship.

Quick Stick Harry ran to the kitchen. He gobbled down his cereal and ran back to his room. He gathered his lacrosse gear and ran outside. He jumped into the car.

Quick Stick Harry was so excited and nervous. He couldn't sit still!

Lax Bro Johnny is Quick Stick Harry's best friend. They play on the same team. Quick Stick Harry's parents gave Lax Bro Johnny a ride to the game.

In the car, Quick Stick Harry asked, "What's up, Bro?"

"Dude, I'm stoked!" said Lax Bro Johnny.

At the field, Quick Stick Harry and Lax Bro Johnny ran over to their team. Coach Gilman called the players together.

"I'm proud of how hard you have worked this year," said Coach Gilman. "I know you can be champions today!"

Ball Hog Billy was on Quick Stick Harry's team. Ball Hog Billy did not like to pass the ball. He wanted to score all the goals.

"Just give me the ball and we will win!" Ball Hog Billy told his team.

"It is important to work hard and play together," Coach Gilman said. "Are you ready?"

"YES!" the whole team yelled.

The players stacked their hands in the middle of the circle. Coach Gilman said, "One, two, three!"

"Mud Dogs!" the players shouted.

Quick Stick Harry and his team jogged out to the field. It was time for the opening face-off!

Quick Stick Harry went to the X in the center of the field. Lax Bro Johnny and Ball Hog Billy went to the wing lines.

The official blew his whistle. "FWEET!"

Quick Stick Harry clamped and scooped the ground ball into his stick. He looked up and passed the ball to Lax Bro Johnny. Quick Stick Harry ran around his defender. He was wide open by the goal.

Lax Bro Johnny passed the ball to Quick Stick Harry. He caught the ball and shot it into the goal. The crowd went wild!

Quick Stick Harry won the next face-off. He passed the ball to Ball Hog Billy.

Ball Hog Billy looked at his open teammates. But he did not pass the ball. He tried to run around one player and then another.

The other team saw that Ball Hog Billy was not going to pass. Two defenders came over to guard him. One defender checked Ball Hog Billy's stick. The ball fell to the ground.

The other team picked up the ball. They passed it down the field. They scored and tied the game.

Ball Hog Billy was upset. He looked over to his parents.

"It's not your fault, Billy," said his mom.

"Your teammates should have been open," said his dad.

Ball Hog Billy kept the ball every time he got it. The other team scored again and again.

Coach Gilman called a timeout. The players ran over with their heads down.

"It's going to be okay, boys," said Coach Gilman. "Just remember to pass the ball!"

Coach Gilman looked at Ball Hog Billy when he said this. Ball Hog Billy put his head down. He knew he was not being a good teammate.

"You can do it, Billy!" said Coach Gilman.

The players ran onto the field. Quick Stick Harry won the next face-off. He passed the ball to Lax Bro Johnny, who passed to Ball Hog Billy.

Ball Hog Billy remembered Coach Gilman's words. He passed the ball to Quick Stick Harry, who took a shot into the goal. SCORE!

The Mud Dogs worked together and tied the game. There were 10 seconds left. The players lined up for the face-off. The boys looked at each other. They knew they could win it right now. The crowd stood up and cheered wildly.

The official blew his whistle.

Quick Stick Harry clamped and scooped the ball into his stick. He passed to Ball Hog Billy, who passed to Lax Bro Johnny. Lax Bro Johnny did a behind-the-back pass to Quick Stick Harry.

Quick Stick Harry caught the ball. He turned to run up the field. Just then, he tripped and dropped the ball.

"Oh no!" he thought. "I have to get it back!"

Ball Hog Billy came out of nowhere. He scooped the ball into his stick. He looked at the goal. He did not have a good shot.

He looked at Quick Stick Harry. He looked at the goal. He looked at his parents. He looked at Coach Gilman. He looked back to Quick Stick Harry.

Suddenly, Lax Bro Johnny shot past like a rocket. Ball Hog Billy passed the ball to him. Lax Bro Johnny caught it. He threw a perfect shot past the goalie. It landed in the upper right corner of the goal. The clock clicked to zero seconds. The game was over!

The fans went wild. The boys piled on each other. The Mud Dogs had won the championship!

Coach Gilman gathered the players.

"I'm proud of all of you," said Coach Gilman. "You are champions today because you worked together as a team!"

He looked at Ball Hog Billy. "From now on, we will call you **Billy the Baller**," said Coach Gilman. "You were a great teammate when it mattered the most. I'm proud of you!"

Quick Stick Harry and Lax Bro Johnny walked over to Quick Stick Harry's parents. "Dude, that was epic!" said Lax Bro Johnny.

"Yeah!" said Quick Stick Harry. "We played as a team and we won! There's only one thing left to do!"

"What's that?" asked Lax Bro Johnny.

"Get some ice cream!" Said Quick Stick Harry.

The End!

Lacrosse Vocabulary Words

ball hog a player who does not pass the ball and always wants to shoot

baller someone who plays a sport and is good at what they do

behind the back any shot or pass that is thrown over the opposite shoulder of the shooting/passing hand

clamp to roll the lacrosse stick over to capture the ball in the back of its head (net)

clear to move the ball from the defensive end of the field to the offensive end

cradling a way of keeping the ball in the lacrosse stick when running

defender a player who works with the goalie to keep the opponent from scoring

face-off when two opposing players face each other at the X at the center of the field and try to win the ball; a face-off happens at the beginning of a game and after each score

Gilman a clear where the goalie or a defender throws the ball as far down the field as possible

goalie the player in the goal who tries to stop opponents from scoring

ground ball a ball that is loose on the ground

lacrosse a team sport played with a lacrosse stick and a lacrosse ball; the oldest organized sport in North America, created by the Native Americans

lax short form of the word "lacrosse"

lax bro short form of the term "lacrosse brothers"; someone who loves the game of lacrosse

official a person (such as a referee or umpire) who makes sure that players follow the rules of a game

quick stick the act of catching and passing or shooting the lacrosse ball in one motion

scoop to pick up the ball using the head of the stick

stick check a legal defensive technique where a player uses his stick to stop an opposing player

Sources for terms of lacrosse
https://beginnerlacrosse.com/terminology
https://laxgoalierat.com/lacrosse-slang/
http://files.leagueathletics.com/Text/Documents/16582/76233.pdf
L is for Lacrosse: An ABC Book by John Sardella

JOHN SARDELLA is the author of three previous books: *How to Start a Successful Youth Lacrosse Program*, *L is for Lacrosse: An ABC Book*, and *A Journey without a Map: Stories of Loss, Grief, and Moving Forward*. John's professional career was spent in the Liverpool CSD. He was a teacher for sixteen years and a principal for fifteen years, and John has been a lacrosse coach for over thirty years. He is now retired and enjoys spending his time writing, golfing, and being with family and friends. John resides in Liverpool, New York, and Naples, Florida. His kids are all grown, and John still sees them often. You can find John on Twitter @ sardella_john, connect via email at ajourneywithoutamap@gmail.com, or visit johnsardella.com.

CPSIA information can be obtained
at www.ICGtesting.com
Printed in the USA
BVHW050926200421
605396BV00010B/2095